What I Saw

poems by JACK McCARTHY

EM PRESS
24041 S Navajo Drive
Channahon, IL 60410
em-press.com

What I Saw

Cover photo by Hank Kaplan
Cover design by Greg Harms
Book design by Brett Neiman
Typeset by Emily Anne Evans
ISBN: 978-0-9850946-4-5

Printed in the United States of America by Total Printing Solutions for EM Press, L.L.C.
First Printing, 2012

"Don't insist on understanding new things, but try with your whole self, with patience, effort and method, to comprehend obvious truths."

—Simone Weil

Table of Contents

The Accommodation: Adam's Recollection 7

Chipmunk Booty Call 11

Magnum Iter 15

Great Catches 24

Red Sweat 27

Phlogiston: Jack McCarthy's Universe 30

The Music I Sometimes Hear a Moment Before Sleep 33

Epithalamion: A Few Words for Kathleen 35

Relativity Made Easy (relatively) 39

What I Saw on My Walk *42*

California Morning 45

The Poem for Hannah 47

The Top 10 Reasons Why I Take Notes at Poetry 49

Fava Beans (& Sour Grapes) 52

24/7 55

Reflections on Retirement or Ode to My Snooze Button 57

After Interviewing Hundreds of Men, Miss Manners Answers All Your Questions About Men's Room Etiquette 60

The Dervish & the Elephant 63

Lucretius on 128 66

They're Dragging the Lake for Dennis 69

A Prayer for John Fernandez 71

British Addresses: An Introduction 75

- Mr. Dick 76
- St. Agnes 77
- Miss L. Wild & Saint Anthony 78
- When Great Detectives Get Together 80
- Goodfellow 82

Cartalk III—the Karma Doors 85

The Death I Was Never Afraid Of 88

When the Cholesterol Catches Up With Me 91

The Accommodation: Adam's Recollection

Adam said to Eve:
Something is happening to me
that I do not understand.

Eve said:
Tell me about it.

Adam said:
I cannot tell you about it
because I do not understand it.

Tell me how it feels.

I'll try, said Adam.
Remember how it felt
when we were in the Garden?
When everything was provided,
ready to our hand?
There was nothing we could want?

The Garden again, said Eve.
I thought we had put that behind us.

Adam said, Oh, we have.
I only bring it up
to talk about the feeling
of having everything I wanted
and only one thing I could do
could screw things up.

Eve looked at Adam—
shaggy beard and matted hair,
his red-rimmed eyes; she knew
he hadn't been sleeping very well;
times in the night she would waken
and know by his breathing,
his occasional sigh,
that he was lying there awake.
But neither of them would speak,
and eventually she'd drift back
into her own fitful sleep. She asked,

This feeling that you have now,
it is like the Garden?

No, no, said Adam.
It is the opposite of that.
It is the feeling of longing for something
so much that everything else means
nothing until I have the thing.
I get filthy and bathe in a clear, cool pool,
and mud and dust come off me,
but I don't feel clean.
I thirst and we find a little stream
and I drink and my thirst is quenched,
but I'm not satisfied.
I hunger and we find fruit and eat,
and my stomach is no longer hungry,
but I still am.
I get tired and we lie down
on cool grass in evening
and I close my eyes,
but I cannot sleep,
because the longing is upon me,
and it is strongest then.

And I know that there is only
one thing that can satisfy it.

Eve had been craving something
undiscovered herself, and hoping
he would have an answer, she asked,
What is the thing you long for?

I do not know.
But it has to do
with your body.

My body.
What is it you want with my body?

I do not know
but I know I'll know it when I find it.

I need to explore you.
I need to figure out what goes where.
I want to do things to you.
I want you to do things to me.

Eve said,
I feel I'm being reduced to something,
but in her heart she thought,
Maybe not Instead of;
maybe In addition to.

Adam said,
Please. I'm begging you.

This, your longing:
when did it become my problem?
Why do I want to get involved?

I do not know. Maybe you don't.
Maybe this is yet another road
down which there is no turning back.
But I perceive that we are in this thing
together, whatever this thing is.
And I can see it's never going to work
unless you help me.

And Eve saw that Adam
was indeed becoming wise,
wise enough to beg for what he needed,
and she felt a strange indulgence,
much of it for him,
and smiled, and touched his matted
hair and said, All right.
I'll accommodate you.
You may explore my body,
and figure out what goes where.
You can do things to me
and I'll do things to you.
But it must be at my time and on my terms,
and you must promise
not to hurt me.

Adam reached up and took
the hand that stroked his hair,
and tried to draw Eve toward him,
but she pulled back, saying,
Not here. Not yet.
First we have to find a pool and bathe.
But this time I'll wash you
and you can wash me.

Adam's fingers had got
interlaced with Eve's
and they rose together
to go looking for a pool,
Adam pulling her along, eyes darting,
Eve stopping now and then to pluck a flower,
yet allowing herself to be drawn along.
Adam thought they should split up,
the quicker to find a pool,
but Eve said No,
this looking was a thing
that they should do together,
and Adam knew he didn't have
the presence of mind
to win an argument.

As they walked, Eve talked
about what just had happened
and they knew it was a new thing,
and needed a name.
They decided to call it "love,"
which in their beginning language meant,
"the state of being in a thing
together."

Chipmunk Booty Call

I was heading south on route 97
and in the opposite lane I saw
a chipmunk dart out in front
of an oncoming car.

He had room to make it,
and the pickup truck in front of me
was already hitting his brakes
to let him cross our lane

but when the chipmunk
turned his head and saw the pickup
he hesitated one fatal second,
then spun and darted back toward home

right under the left front wheel of
the northbound car. It seemed to me that
I could hear his tiny body pop.
As I sped past the little mess I yelled,

"Idiot!" because I can never
resist adding insult to injury.
But a brief reflection put me more
in sympathy with the chipmunk.

The day was March second, the sun
higher in the sky than it had been since
Columbus Day; in the chipmunk calendar
maybe it was spring, Exploration Day,

and this dude who'd survived the winter
on the east side of the road
was being impelled by the big urges
that small animals feel in spring.

Yeah, the more I thought
about it the surer I became
that he was crossing the road
for sex.

Chip would have been
better off living like a monk,
but it was in the interest of
the *species* that he venture out.

And then I started thinking about
all the stupid things that I myself have done
in pursuit of the elusive booty
all the chances I've taken in the name of love.

The time in '64 I hitchhiked to New York
on the off-chance that in a city of eight million,
I might bump into one in particular;
hey, I knew she was there.

1988, the 17 years of my first marriage behind me,
the woman at the Coolidge Corner Theatre
who laughed in all the right, sexy places
of Unbearable Lightness of Being;

I went back at the same time
Sunday after Sunday night,
hoping to hear her laugh again,
to recognize her in the flickering light.

There was the barefoot girl with the amazing
backside that I followed the entire lovely
undulating width of the Dartmouth campus
one gorgeous summer day in 1966.

Research on frogs shows that
attracting males has nothing to do
with the female's appearance or secretions,
it's totally dependent on the way

her tail moves. Asked what was
the first thing he noticed about a woman,
I think it was Bogie who said,
"Depends which way she's going."

Then I think about the time I pontificated
to a small group that in this day and age,
before you lie down with a new partner
you should demand a doctor's certificate first,

and they all laughed at me. Correctly,
because in these affairs you have to
recognize the point of no return.
Chip's mistake was turning back.

Not a failure
of judgment, a failure of nerve.
And if *our* chipmunk didn't make it, well,
there was probably another one that did.

Sure, it's dangerous,
but the species *will* perpetuate itself.
I want you to think of this
every time you see a chipmunk.

A while back I heard a comedienne
talking about those condom ads
on the subway that say, "It Isn't
Worth Risking Your Life,"

how those ads make a lot of sense
at eight o'clock on Monday morning,
but at night when decisions get made,
it really sort of *is* worth it.

I wonder if chipmunks mate for life;
maybe had that little guy made it
across the road that one time,
he never would have had to cross again.

I'm glad I'm out of all that madness now.
Once you're safely ensconced
on the west side of that highway,
things still get messy sometimes,

love is by its nature messy—
my favorite feminist anthem of the 80s
was "I Ain't Sleepin' on the Wet Spot No More."
Still, from the west side you look

down from Olympus at all the lives being risked
just for the sake of the little tickle in the loins,
and you forget all the chances you took
to get where you are

including that maddest gamble of all,
the longshot wager that you'll always want
to be with this person you're with today.
Always is *such* a long word.

But there I go, falling for the rhetoric,
the Big Lie about the Little Tickle,
when we all know that when it's happening,
it's the biggest thing in the world.

The species *will* perpetuate itself.
Why did the chipmunk cross the road?
Because for one brief shining moment,
he stopped being a chicken.

Magnum Iter

I. We were ripe for intimidation
and the most inimitable intimidator
of all was Mister Hatch. He taught
Latin and his classroom was right
next the marble portal inscribed
Huc venite pueri ut viri sitis—
"Come this way, boys, that you may be men."
The road to manhood ran past Mister Hatch.

He was the legend of legends.
To pass his room when Latin I
was getting out—the door bursts open
and fourteen boys of wildly various sizes
various amounts of ankle showing
explode into the corridor
some of them in tears.
There they mill

like survivors of a terrorist bomb,
oblivious to traffic patterns, and to
passersby who haven't shared their
ordeal, comparing desperate notes—
"What did he say the homework was?"
"When do we have to have that memorized?"
"*My brother—did my brother make it out?*
Has anybody seen my brother?"

What was so terrifying about him?
He was not a big man.
Refereeing a lacrosse game
he looked a tough enough little guy
all bulbs and wire
but nothing out of Stephen King.
Knobby knees and calf muscles, forehead,
but I doubt he weighed one-forty.

But put a sportcoat on him, close
him in that little room with us and he'd
bolt up and start to pace behind us
like a lion from the Serengeti loose
in a stableful of calves tethered

round an oval table unable to turn
their head, never knowing when
and where he might strike.

What *was* terrifying was his voice. Rumor
had it he'd been gassed in World War I.
In soft registers that voice was like
the whisper of a bullfrog, sometimes hard
to hear—which in itself was menacing—
inevitably, any uncaught word
came back to haunt you, and ask him
to repeat himself? Oh come now.

In loud registers, his voice was
lion's roar, not challenge, but a feral
non-negotiable demand for submission
the assertion of one species' absolute
power of life and death over another.
It didn't trigger adrenalin but
paralysis. In its middle registers—
no, his voice *had* no middle registers.

Each class was like a Bach organ piece
that started soft, one hand weaving
gentle melody fraught with inevitability
promise that before we're finished here
every key, every pedal, every stop
will have been exploited for maximum
dramatic and emotional effect, that
I am going to put you through

the wringer. Most terrifying of
all was the certainty that if
you had left just one thing undone
he would find you out
there was no place to hide
in that little room, there
wasn't enough cannon
fodder, it might take almost

all of his allotted fifty
minutes but the undone task would
rise like a bubble to the surface
sit there calling, "*Mister Ha-atch*"
till he would wheel on you and you
would regret your oversight like
Troy regretted letting in that horse.
Once that door shut and locked us in

with him all that we could ever
be to each other was potential
decoys in this little herd
if he took you tonight
he might not get to me
so what if you were my best friend.
This was the optimum in training
for the corporate world.

I don't remember so much
the content of what he would say
when he caught you out
but it felt like, gently, "Why
don't you know
the present subjunctive of *sum*
Mr. McCarthy?"
"I don't know sir."

"We've already established *that* you don't
know I was asking *why* you don't know."
"I don't know why I don't know, sir."
"Wasn't it the most important
thing in the world last night?"
"Of course it was sir."
Then a little more forcefully,
"*Have you ever in your life been asked to do*

anything more important than memorize
the present subjunctive of the verb to be?"
"No sir." Then bellowing,
like the Minotaur
thundering toward you

from every direction of the Labyrinth
"THEN HOW COULD YOU NOT HAVE DONE IT?"
"I DON'T KNOW SIR!"

And I was one of the lucky ones.
I didn't have Mr. Hatch till senior year
Latin IV Special. We were *quam optimi*,
as good as it got. We had learned our chops in
the less surreal classrooms of the Stuckeys,
and the Galbreaths, and the Coffins, and we
knew our stuff or we wouldn't have been there.
And if he treated preps as *barbari*

for the simple reason they did not know
Latin, he respected us because we did.
Not that we didn't at times disappoint him—
times his outrage was compounded by
knowledge we had come so far, that this
once-great school had fallen on such evil times
that Mr. McCarthy could arrive in this class
without knowing the meaning of *vereor*—

(wheeling) which means what, Mr. Gates?
"I am terrified, sir." "Correct."
Did Gates really know?
or had he gotten lucky?
We had Mister Hatch at 5:25,
after sports, at the end of a long day
when we thought we were almost home free.
I remember that room always being dark.

There'd be a lamp on over his desk
and a floor lamp somewhere
but I don't think he ever
turned on the overhead light
and entering that room in the dark
months between October and April
was like entering the lair of a predator
who smelled like floor-wax and old books.

But we were the favored sons
and whole classes could pass
without a spark catching his fuse.
Once even this: I was translating
a passage about the Cyclops, and the Latin
had alliteration, so I went for it
in my English, passing up the obvious
"His feet struck the grass," for

the marginally more ambitious "smote the sod,"
and Mr. Hatch said, "You have..."
in that way he had of beginning a phrase
before he had really had time to gather
the entirety of his fragmented voice
and we all froze because we knew that
when he was moved enough to do that
the *fasces* was about to fall

and he went on
"...the *nicest* way of coming up
with just the right phrase in translation..."
and we sat there stunned.
I stammered, "Thank you, sir" and risked
a glance across the table at flabbergasted
faces, Barzun, Lenesse, and Marcus
their bodies rigid

their breath still indrawn
nobody knowing what to do with this
totally uncharacteristic lapse
somehow more frightening
than anything he'd ever done before.
It was probably from that moment I was
fated to teach prep school Latin
a few years myself.

II. That fall my mother died
and in adolescent bravado I
promised my father I'd get
Highest Honors for the fall term
something I'd never been able to do.
I worked hard, would have made it
except Mr. Hatch gave me a B-plus
instead of the A-minus I had earned.

I dared approach him and he told me
he'd deducted for some lines of poetry
I'd failed to memorize. I wailed,
"But that was extra credit,"
and he painstakingly explained,
like astronomy to a small child,
"You can't expect extra credit if
there's no deduction if it's *not* done."

Then, sensing the depth of my disappointment,
he surprised me, offered, "Is there some
reason this grade's important to you?"
But I hadn't come looking for charity
and I said no, left quickly so he wouldn't
know I cried. In March, when my classmates
were deep into their Aeneid papers,
my father died.

Returned to school I tried to
weasel out of the paper, arguing
I couldn't concentrate, I was
worried about things at home,
what would become of my brother?
But Mister Hatch didn't buy it,
so I ended up throwing together
over two all-nighters

a collage of quotes
transcribed from impeccable sources
but too obviously selected
for their extravagant length.
He gave me D-minus, which let me graduate,

but brought me down to C-plus for the year
(though it did not deny me
third place on the Latin prize exam.)

The next few years got ugly fast.
I dropped out of Dartmouth, went
down a labyrinth or two of my own
devising. Maybe someday it will be of
benefit to remember even those things.
I came out the other side and at
twenty-five was back at Dartmouth
taking Latin and writing, finally,

an Aeneid paper good enough for
presentation to the Classics Club.
The central insight of that paper
was supported by my discovery that
in the first six books Aeneas weeps
fourteen times; in the last six, once.
A demonstrative, emotional Phrygian
becomes a stoic, Augustan Roman,

culminating in his *Disce puer* speech
to his son: "Learn from me, boy, about duty,
about doing the right thing always.
You'll have to learn from someone else
about happiness." Mister Hatch,
retired from Exeter and living in Vermont,
was at the Classics Club that night.
I introduced my paper with the story

of the Exeter D-minus, ending,
"Mister Hatch, this paper is for you.
I apologize for being eight years late."
I had survived, and I had come to
love him. I've always felt that was
the year that I became a man, never quite
known why; now, having told this story,
I suspect that might have been the night.

III. *Huc venite pueri ut viri sitis.*
What did it mean, really? Never
would we be men *unless* we came
this way? It frightened me
the first time that I read it,
as though I knew intuitive my way
to manhood would be terrible indeed.
I always preferred the side door

of that building, uninscribed,
unpromising, unthreatening.
But some read that inscription
and declined to enter at all.
Others came, but disappeared along
the way. For some the obstacle
was Mister Hatch's class, to
"*Did my brother make it out?*"

the answer was No. Yet surely they
all came to manhood too. On different
timetables, by different routes.
If we survive the terrorism of
our very maleness, we arrive.
Sometimes working phonathons
I get a man confides, "I only
stayed at Exeter a month,

but I still like to give something,"
and I feel a special gratitude to him,
but at the same time embarrassment,
as though inadvertently I've raised
some ancient shame.
I want to ask him,
"Was it Mister Hatch?"
I want to tell him, "Yes,

we were a hard proud lot, who
came that way and who survived."
Nobody called you a deserter
but neither did Latin have a phrase
for "conscientious objector."

You took the road less travelled by,
and how much difference, really,
did it make?

Magnum iter is an idiom;
it looks like "great journey,"
but it translates "forced march."
We were on a *magnum iter*.
Sometimes in the long dark nights
of those marches, we abandoned
our *impedimenta*, the softnesses
within us that were destined

not to serve us in the coming
battle with *barbari*, who would
have every advantage over us except
virtus, the stuff of manhood. We had to
leave some of our *comites* to fend for
themselves by roads in enemy territory.
Today when we look back we see only
a great journey and a victory

not a forced march
never the casualties.
But the issue never was
that we *be* men, it was
the kind of men we should become.
And I want somehow to apologize
for all of us to the man
who left after a month.

And I want to ask if he
by any chance remembers seeing,
back beside the road
he didn't take,
any of my *impedimenta*,
my brother, or the last
promise I made
to my father.

Great Catches

Great catches? Well the second year that I
was in computers, there was one I made.
Programming was playing Operations.
A grudge match. We were mostly college grads
and operators weren't. Each side believed,
and not without some cause, their lives would be
serene but for the gross incompetence
and almost criminal negligences
of the other.

We were up eight to two.
It was a couple of years I hadn't played
and I was galloping around left field
for just the joy of running. Everyone
was having a good laugh about me, at
me, with me—who can say why people laugh?

The fifth inning they started to come back.
Now it was eight to five and they had two
on and two out. You know how one team gets
quiet sometimes? That was us. Then this guy
unloads one toward the alley in left-center.
I give it one look and I'm off, full speed.
He was big and I liked the way he stood,
so I was playing deep enough; I just
didn't know if I could cover all that ground.

I ran and ran. When I looked up again,
my God, it was the kind of chance you pray for,
the one that's maybe at your very limit,
Willie Mays off Vic Wertz in fifty-four,
or Evans off Joe Morgan in Game Six.
I really hadn't thought that I could get there;
now what if, having gotten there, I blew it?

I stretched my glove-hand toward the ball,
careering downward, outward. I could see
the lazy back-rotation of the stitches.
Right then in happened that the ball and I
had come so far, our relative position
to the poles had swung ninety degrees.

The setting sun, which had been somewhere
down the right-field line when I started out,
was shining now right square into my eyes,
and for the next few seconds I was blind.

I did what Mays or Evans would have done:
I stuck my glove out where the ball should come.
It happened in this instance I guessed right.
I felt it penetrate the pocket of the glove,
jar my arm a little by its impact,
seat itself as firmly as a rivet,
stop spinning and give over its momentum
entirely to me.

The noise was instant,
spontaneous loud release of tension,
the rebel yells of Yankees who wore ties
all day, backslapping congratulation
that's so obnoxious to the other side,
that's half of why we do it. We got back up
and scored a bunch of runs, and they never
got close to striking distance again.

There came a time that winter when I had
to work all night, even going down to sit
in the computer room while my job ran—
repeatedly, because I made mistakes.
The operator kept eying me. At length
he asked, "Are you the guy that made that catch?"
I said, "What catch was that?" He said, "You know.
The softball game on the Fenway last June."
"Oh, that catch. Yuh, I guess so, that was me."
"It was a good catch," he says, and turning
to the console, runs my jobs without complaint.

All my catching may go back to a day
when I was eight, or maybe nine, which would
have made my brother Leo two or three,
the age when he was always taking off.
One time the cops caught him a mile from home,
on Savin Hill Avenue, running barefoot

down the sidewalk with his future in front
of him and a load in his pants behind,
trailing the rope that had restricted him
to the back yard—a little while at least.

This was another day, and we were trapped
indoors by bitter winter weather, Leo,
our sister Judy, and myself. It might
have been New Year's Day. I have a feeling
I was making them listen to football,
which I didn't like much on the radio,
but there was this, that they disliked it more—
one of the crueler pleasures of being
oldest. I was sitting in the armchair
inmost in the room, nearest the radio,
furthest from the draft. Leo climbed up the back
of another armchair, one that stood in front
of a third floor window that looked down on
the sidewalk and a barren little patch
of frozen, stony ground that wasn't yard,
just interstice between house and pavement.

His chair began to tip. Leo went, "Aaaaah—"
and continued to fall. His head broke through
the window, and he kept falling. Judy
screamed. I don't remember thinking, and I
don't remember moving, I just remember
being there, grabbing him around the legs.
I wasn't strong enough to pull him back.
"Mum. Dad. Help." From another room, they came.
They pulled him back.

They're long gone now. There was
no catching them. Leo has been dead ten years.
He never remembered, and Judy doesn't
either. Maybe it really didn't happen.
But my guess is it did—and that I was
reliving it in every game of ball
I ever played, with every halfway
difficult running catch I ever made.

Red Sweat

One night when I got home from work my wife told me
my red sweatshirt had been stolen off the clothesline
and I got mad the way you do when someone takes
your stuff. As if there were a hundred degrees of
anger: think of one degree as when the remote
control doesn't work right away and you have to
lean a little forward and zap it one more time.
Toward the high end of the scale is, oh, ninety-five,
where you want to kill someone, not just have them killed,
but you'd still like to lay the groundwork for getting
away with it. At ninety-nine you no longer
care if you get away with it. I don't know what
a hundred is like. I've never experienced
a hundred. Maybe spontaneous combustion.

In the moment it took to let my sweatshirt go,
what I was feeling was maybe thirty degrees
of anger—over the twenty-five bucks, the ten
days it would take to mail-order a replacement.
But seconds later I had shot to ninety-nine.
I didn't hurt my wife or kids, but I pictured
picking up a chair and crashing it down against
the gas stove, to see how much damage I could do—
nothing against chair or stove; they were just handy.

I hated feeling this way. If someone had come
along, some knacker of disordered emotions,
some entrepreneur of amok, and said, "Jack, if
you write me a check for a thousand dollars, I'll
take away this feeling right now," I would have done
it, and left the money-worry for tomorrow.
All over a twenty-five dollar sweatshirt. Red.

Somehow I had the presence of mind to think, "Wait
a minute. How'd we get to ninety-nine so quick?
What happened to all the numbers in between? Fast
forward?" I tried to reconstruct my train of thought.

The first thought that occurred to me had been about
the Mafia: that they don't send people into
Dorchester to score sweatshirts off of clotheslines. No,
this was an inside job. This tog had been taken
by someone in the neighborhood. Okay, I can
deal with that. We're simmering about thirty-five.

My second thought was that a sweatshirt is something
you wear outdoors, not in. And what with my jogging,
walking the kids to the library, et cetera,
I spend a lot of time out on the street in this
neighborhood. Those things being so, eventually
I will bump into the kid who stole my sweatshirt,
and he'll be wearing it. Thirty edges upward.

The next scene plays out like this in the war room of
my cerebellum: I assert, "That's my sweatshirt,"
and the kid makes some smart answer, and I don't know
what to say

so I have to kill him. And Bingo:
straight to ninety-nine. Do not pass Go, do not collect
two hundred dollars. I reflected that it takes
a thoughtful man to get as angry as I do.
That recognition didn't make my anger go
away. But a friend came by and we went somewhere
together. When feelings careen out of control,
friends help steer. I laughed at something ridiculous
and something serious released inside. When your
feelings own you, laughter redeems.

But there were still
a lingering several degrees of resentment
sticking like last fall's leaves in my emotional
gutters, blowing into the dark storm sewer of
resident anger that makes some of us wake up
day in, day out at about seven and a half.
At times, when we make love-not-war there's a moment
when we catch a glimpse of zero; you can hear us
calling to it sometimes in the night, O, O, O.
The best we ever go unaccompanied to
bed is somewhere between eighteen and forty-five.

This residue stayed with me several months, till one
day I was jogging Ashmont Street and a young man
that I'd always liked walked by. "Hi Mr. McCarthy."
"Hi John." When I was three or four steps past, I stopped
and thought, "That was my sweatshirt," and I remembered
the winter John's crazy mother kicked him out, and
he was sleeping in the cellars of three-deckers
in the neighborhood, and he must have been cold.
I didn't even turn around. I just went back
to my jogging, feeling about ten pounds lighter.

Phlogiston: Jack McCarthy's Universe

for my first wife, the mother of my daughters

Early scientists observed
that when wood burned, the ash
weighed more than what they'd started with.
They'd seen the fire eating at the substance;
they'd watched the gray smoke
form, and rise, and curl toward heaven;
they believed that what was gone
was element whose weight was negative.
They named this element "*phlogiston*,"
which means, "that which gets burned away."

An element with negative weight:
I love that explanation for
the brilliance of its wrongness.
Today we know that fire is oxidation,
just like rust on an old car
(although rust is too slow
for the eye to know the change
that's taking place: not eating,
but patient encroaching of the space
by something uninvited).

You and I started
with so much going for us.
I thought I was so good
I'd never have to compromise
and you bought it.
Did we love each other?
We believed we did;
maybe it's the same.

Gradually the empirical data
suggested I might have to
give some ground
on some peripheral issues
but certainly not on anything
substantial.

We sensed something we couldn't see.
We weighed the evidence
of phenomenal children.
"A bad tree cannot bear good fruit,"
we quoted to each other. But maybe
there's a mercy in the universe
that makes occasional exceptions
to even the most rigid rule.
"Anomalies," we call them now.

And we weren't really a *bad* tree.
More like a Rubik's cube
we reconfigured relentlessly
till finally just one square
was out of place.

Science today believes in anti-matter:
for every particle there exists
an equal other, with opposite charge.
When paired particles come together
they become pure energy.
Tempting to think of energy as love;
but particles can't combine
unless the match is perfect.

Compromise was an understatement in the end.
I hung out a sign that said For Sale,
discreet at first, as on a home in Wellesley,
but eventually more like a police auction
of rusty cars abandoned over parking tickets,
going each to some uncontested bidder
interested only for the parts.

Our particles came apart then,
fled in opposite directions;
what little energy was left dissipated.
To each of us it seemed
the other was become anti-matter,
detectable only in cloud chambers.

I started this poem as one more attempt
to make you hear me say I'm sorry—
and I am, sorry that it ever seemed to you
that the place your life went down with me
was black hole.

But even if we didn't get
the Big Bang for our buck,
well maybe at the heart of creation is a fire
and wrong-headed as our theories might have been,
they weren't wrong-hearted,
and they did get us close to that fire
for a little while
as the universe measures things.

Now, even with your feelings set
carefully in the balance,
I cannot say that we were wrong to try.
Maybe what got burned away
was of negative weight,
the freight of illusion—phlogiston;
and the fire did
keep several people warm.

High-school teachers centuries from now
will tell their students how
we in the last millennium believed
in something we called "anti-matter,"
and the kids will laugh
and wait for teacher to tell them
what they can believe in now.

The Music I Sometimes Hear a Moment Before Sleep

I'd always liked the piece—melodic, sweet;
but no more than so many things we do.
It never gave me goose-bumps till the Sunday
I decided just to mouth the words
the first time through.

In my own silence I could better hear
Carole's sweet alto in front on my left,
Tim's lavish Irish tenor on my right.
Then when I did come in, my own voice sounded
deep, rich, sudden, almost scaring me
to silence, but instead it sang itself
even a little deeper in me, stronger,
till Carole and Michelle, who always waited here,
followed with the echo. Jean brought her intuitive
high harmony, and out of nowhere Tim decided
he would "goof around," the way he sometimes does
in practice, never Mass, inventing for himself a part
about two notes below the melody, which Anne
was carrying an octave up from me, all of us
riding along on Terry's guitar. And electricity
began a slow, pagan, sensual crawl up my legs
from the white marble of the altar.

Seconds later it was over, and I sighed
and looked out at the pews, and wondered why
their mouths weren't hanging open—hadn't they
heard what we just did? Tim whispered, as he
has every Sunday since, "God, that was good."

Sometimes it makes me think of my divorce—
taking myself out to make things better.
I thought for a year that it had worked that way;
till Bridget followed me out, and moved in
at sixteen with her boyfriend to a basement
in South Boston where they both could throw
their stuff all on the floor. Still, she went on
to graduate from Dartmouth (happy, yes; ending, no).
Siobhan stayed on, but went her own hard way
of run-ins with the law, eventually

let drop about the four years that she ran
on Dexatrim, when nobody was home
to watch her eat. She too survived, and won
a scholarship to Bowdoin College.
She said the food was great, and we believed her.
Kerry, who always seemed the most at risk:
she was the one who never missed a beat.
She won a ticket to the Ivy League too.
Someday she'll write a fine story
about all this from Kerry's point of view.

And by the way, I asked my daughters how
they felt about my using their details
as fodder for this poem. They were not
reluctant, hinting gently that it might however be
improved by something more poetic than
mere academic fact, financial aid solutions.

Perhaps my brood of critics has it right.
But something in me apprehends these facts
as dactyls in a larger poetry, in which each
absence is as critical as every presence, as
necessary as rests to notes in a musical score.
Mine are the squiggly things, and little hats;
the sharps, the clefs, the naturals; the flats.
If such a poetry exists, I'd like to tap in to it;
and one of these details might be
the master password lets me do it.
And someone, somewhere, might say,
"That was good."

Epithalamion: A Few Words for Kathleen

(the Boston College edit)

We're here today to celebrate
the wedding of Kathleen and Mark.

Kathleen, when she was eight years old,
started coming with me to my Friday night meetings.
That group had really good coffee,
and as she made her way time after time to
the coffeepot, I'd lose sight of Kathleen because she was short,
but I could follow her progress by watching the heads turn
to bless her with their eyes as she passed,
beautiful child that she was.

At the break they'd raffle off a Big Book,
and when the meeting broke up, Kathleen
would go from table to table collecting
all the discarded raffle tickets, which she would
bring home and store in a shoebox.
Why? I never figured it out.

Up came my anniversary, and my sponsor
was out of town, so I asked Kathleen
if she'd be willing to say a few words
in front of a roomful of grownups and she was game—
Kathleen was always game. She had to stand
on a chair to reach the microphone,
and if I remember right, what she said was,
"It is always an occasion when someone celebrates
their eleventh anniversary. Jack?"

And if I'd been expecting something
a little more—what? personal? still,
it was a great beginning for a ten-year run.

The next year she didn't need to stand on the chair,
and she wrote a poem that began,
"My dad is the best/he's been that way since birth/
It's a shame there's only one of him/on the planet earth."

Year three she brought Annie with her, and she said,
"Last year I read a poem for my dad's anniversary.
This year we're here to explain the poem."
Oh, would that every poet might acknowledge
that responsibility.

Kathleen's presence those Friday nights lit up
that big gymnasium, and a lot of people
who never got to watch their own kids grow up
came to look forward to her presentations
as a highlight of their year.

Tom G., who couldn't come with us
when we put on meetings in prisons
because he always set off the metal detectors—
because he had a police bullet lodged
inoperably close to his spine—
said to me one night, "That kid is the best
advertisement for this program that anyone could ever see."
And Billy T., a former three-hundred pound biker,
told me that he had a daughter Kathleen's age—
"somewhere"—and that every year he cried at
her presentation—but it was the *good* crying.

Now it's my turn to say a few words for Kathleen—
but she's tied my hands a little,
made me promise not to make *her* cry.

So I'll address my words first to the community,
then to the groom.

The ceremony required that I go through
the motions of giving Kathleen away.
That was, at best, polite fiction. It's been
said that our children are like arrows:
for them to reach their marks, we have to let
them go. Kathleen is an arrow that was loosed
a long time ago. Or maybe more like
a Hail Mary pass lofted from midfield
while the Miami stands are chanting "4-3-2...."

I'm one happy father to see Mark standing
in the end zone with hands like Gerard Phelan.

Still, most fathers of the bride, if they were honest,
would admit that they don't think there's a young man
in the world who's worthy of their little girl.
I want Mark to know that I don't
feel that way—   particularly.

But what I'm sure of is that Kathleen and Mark
have been extraordinarily lucky to find each other,
especially in Mary Ann's.
It's crazy out there, most of us feel fortunate
to find *anyone* willing to cast their lot with us,
let alone the *right* person. Today my heart
is telling me that this is right.

Now, Mark, about the dowry.
I'm afraid I have to ask to be dispensed
from that particular archaic tradition;
it's not that I'm ungenerous, just unemployed.

But somewhere among Kathleen's belongings,
in a cellar or an attic or at the bottom of a closet,
you might still find a shoebox full of raffle tickets
that didn't win anything.

If you find it, Mark, hang onto it.
A lot of hopes went into that box,
the hopes of people whose last names I never knew,
people who didn't win life's lotteries,
didn't dodge all of life's bullets,
who once looked at Kathleen and took heart,
who loved her and left their tickets on the tables
in hope that they might be for her
tickets to a better life than they had had.

And any time you feel that life's too hard,
and you're too much alone,
take that box out, run your fingers

through those old raffle tickets.
Mix them up real good, and think about
how much luck it takes
to find the one person in the world
that we were meant to find.

Then go to the kitchen and put on a pot
of some really good coffee—
and make enough
for two.

Relativity Made Easy (relatively)

for Carol

I know a guy who once got pulled over
on his way home from a pot party.
Cop: “Know how fast you were going?”
Guy: “Forty? Forty-five?”
Cop: “Four.”

That story got me interested in relativity.
One corollary holds we’re driven by electron clocks,
as if somewhere in the body is a cylinder,
submicroscopic, with an electron bouncing
at the speed of light—whhsshht, ba-dip,
hitting the hard, flat, top of the cylinder,
whhsshht, ka-chung, straight back to the bottom,
over and over, a million times a second,
gazillion times a year, superball fired
from the atomic cannon of the Big Bang,
whhsshht, ba-dip, whhsshht, ka-chung.

And if we somehow make
those ba-dips and ka-chungs slow down,
we see ourselves and the world as
rushing toward each other faster and faster.

But the longer we wait, the more
they slow down of their own accord,
as part of getting older.

In eighth grade I was ba-dipping
and ka-chunging so fast that
social studies class went on forever.
Summer vacation gaped in front of me,
an infinity of sun-bleached, barefoot,
salt-rimed possibility, September invisible,
light years beyond my event-horizon.
Last summer it was Labor Day before
I realized I hadn’t been to the beach yet.
My perception of time is still set
to the old ba-dips and ka-chungs,
but my whhsshhts are half a century slower.

And this same principle applies to marriages.
When you're just starting out, your whole
long future is at stake, and so much
that can go wrong—career, health, children,
Sure, you love each other now,
but the people that you'll be in twenty years
how will *they* feel about each other?

And the tighter the two of you are in the beginning,
the more you're doomed to magnify
the little differences come up between you.

The world saw my first wife and me
as two peas, agreed on almost everything.
But in our supercollider pod,
the operative word was "almost,"
which evolved into "irreconcilable differences."

This marriage is all different, it feels like
infinite space here, collisions are rare.
But space is curved, and if we miss
each other now and again, hey,
what goes around comes around.
You don't hold me responsible for your orbits,
and you don't try to dictate mine.

And measured in ba-dips and ka-chungs,
the stakes just aren't as high. If we hit
a bad patch it can never seem as long
as one of Mr. Barry's science classes.
We could live a long, long time together,
but it would be a time of ever-shorter summers.
Daisy Buchanan said she always looked forward
to the longest day of the year,
but then she always missed it.
You and I miss whole seasons,
but somehow we have made of this
a relative advantage.

It would take a lot of
whhsshht, ba-dip, whhsshht, ka-chungs
for us to outrun the expanding universe
we grant each other,
and we just don't have that many left.

If we take the sixth grade science
out of that statement, I think
what I just said was
I'll love you till I die.

What I Saw on My Walk

What did I see on my walk this morning?
I saw no bears or cougars; I did see
flyers about them (though I sometimes think
they post those more to attract than to warn off).

I didn't see any hawks or eagles—
not that I expected to, at that hour;
the early bird might get the worm, but
he won't catch many thermals at first light.

And this morning I didn't see any coyotes.
I thought I would; later than I was out today,
I've seen them in the meadow
that runs alongside the trail, hunting
in that cartoonish way they have
of leaping up and coming down with all
four feet together to try to disable mouse
or mole or shrew or vole—whatever morsel
is on their coyote breakfast menu.
We've seen them do that even
while they pay absolutely no attention
to the roosters crowing and the hens
clucking in the pens anent the meadow.

So no, this morning I did not have one of those
eerie visions of coyote crossing the trail
in front of me, just barely visible through
the morning mist, like a ghost predator;
nor one of those eye-locked silent interactions
in which I try to reassure psychically that I am
not a credible threat while coyote gazes back
at me and seems to ponder whether
I'm decrepit enough to be edible yet.

What *did* I see on my walk this morning?
One rabbit, and him I almost missed,
as I whispered silent prayers to myself
and to whom or whatever else might have
attended; not religion any more, nor yet quite
superstition; someone has friended me
who's coined the term "spiritual suspicions,"

and I now see that my prayer
fits well that general description.

And I did see a deer, a big buck, but that
wasn't technically on my walk, I was already
in the car en route home when I spotted him
in the field across the road just north of where
the trail crosses. There was no one behind me
so I pulled over and parked on the shoulder
and got out to look at him. He was on
the far side of the field, some fifty yards away,
which he must have felt a safe distance,
because for two minutes or so
he just stood there, very still,
and we eyed each other.
Then the traffic picked up
and I went back to the car.

What did I see on my walk this morning?
That was about it, for wild things.
There was one other thing you'd probably
like to hear about; along the lines
of that old swayback horse that every time
we see it out in its pasture you say,
"Somebody must really love that horse."

There was this old woman—
when I say old, I'm saying my age,
give or take a few; possibly as young
as you; I thought not, but in that range.
The old woman had a leash in one hand
leading a retriever, no longer golden, clearly older
in dog years than either of us, laboring
a little, but enjoying, as goldens so obviously
do, every aspect of this morning constitutional.

The old woman with her other hand
was pulling a child's red rusted wagon
in which rode a second no longer
golden retriever, this one even older,
perhaps the mother of the one she led,

and able to do not much more than
lift its head to smell whatever cinemascope
high definition three-D summer blockbuster
olfactory spectacle it is dogs so enjoy—

and I knew this woman understood that
dogs gets their kicks from their sense of smell
and she had somehow lifted-prodded-cajoled-
maneuvered-leveraged her no-longer-golden retriever
up into her car and from there down into that
little red wagon, so that even though it couldn't
walk any more, and—who knows—
maybe couldn't even see or hear—
it could still smell the rabbits and coyotes,
rooster and chickens, birds and other dogs—
maybe even deer and cougar and black bear—
all those smells that were about all the adventure
that old dog was still capable of.

What, my darling, did I see on my walk
this morning? I saw love.

California Morning

Under a hot white August sky
I was sitting on my new sister-in-law's deck
looking out over a ravine
savoring my first cup of coffee
and three hours time difference
calling what I was doing "meditating"
which meant that nobody would bother me
when a coyote appeared
ambling up a path out of the ravine
in my general direction.

A rabbit popped out of the brush between us
saw the coyote
nothing between them but fast lane
froze into his clump of brown grass imitation.

Coyote stopped too although he gave
no indication he had seen the rabbit.
No, it was some rare quality in
the morning air he stayed to savor.

Over the next ten minutes coyote got interested
in creatures and events invisible to me
at every compass point
except the rabbit's
took maybe a dozen steps
none of them actually toward his
motionless potential breakfast special
yet each oblique step
narrowing the distance between them
by a margin discernible only
to an old geometry teacher

till suddenly
on no trigger I could see
maybe just some natural version
of a three-second violation—
it ain't that you're too close
but it's been too long
since you been far enough away—

breakfast beat a fast break
back into the brush
and coyote
never a look after him
resumed his stroll
as if knowing all along
it was too much to hope for
but hey

it's a numbers game
and sometimes
after all the indirection
sometimes
just often enough to keep you coming back
you *do nail something just right*.
I lifted my cup in toast to a *poet*.

The Poem for Hannah

A reading at the Bookcellar one June:
at the break a woman came up to me,
fortyish, refined, lovely; something odd,
unfocused, about her eyes. She told me
she was legally blind, the written word
was little use to her; she wondered did
I have a tape? I wondered to myself
if she knew how lovely she was. Aloud
I said that I had neither tape nor book
to sell, nor any prospect imminent.

That was when she told about the daughter
who had inherited her damaged sight;
how she was always looking for the means
to pass on her own love for poetry.

I have daughters, too, all grown up now,
inheritors from me of certain traits:
bad Irish teeth, the volcanic skin of
adolescence; maybe the other A-disease,
the dream-coat I connived to wrestle from
the still-warm corpus of my own father...

I thought about guilt that comes of watching
children suffer consequence of things that
were our legacy to them the very
moment of the ecstasy of effort,
moment everything seemed to be going
about as well as it ever does go.
When Jesus said the sins of the fathers
would be visited upon the children,
he wasn't cursing us with anything,
he was just making an observation
on a sad inevitability.

Chatting with the woman at the reading,
my mind went out to something in my car,
the tape I used to memorize poems.
I told her I could copy that for her,
would she be interested? and she said
yes, enthusiastic. The woman's name

was Hannah, which as it happens was my
mother's name, dead then almost forty years,
the corpus of her work a bureau drawer
of unpublished stories, cedar-smelling,
moldering somewhere in a landfill now.

"Poems for Hannah" was conceived that night.
Sixty minutes of my best, one or two
cassettes a week, tape click audible
each time I took a drink, or cleared my throat.
High-speed dubbing—weekends with the Munchkins.
But when people asked if I had something
to sell, I didn't have to disappoint.

My one regret's I didn't write this poem
before I made the tape, as dedication,
to say, Hannah, these are my children now,
these poems; imperfect. In them you'll find
every flaw and failing that's in me.
But as with children also, there are times
and places that I know myself exceeded,
hear my own voice tell truths I never knew
I knew. There's something more at work here than
the hard-earned chips I came to table with—
and the ecstasy *is* in the effort,
always.

And if all that's left at the end's
a bureau drawer of stories carelessly
misplaced and lost even by the few who
loved us, or a tape of the most privileged
moments of grace of one's life, recorded
on an obsolete technology; if
there are no children *except* wounded ones,
still you and I are right to roll the dice.
Nothing, otherwise, shows that we were here;
nothing, otherwise, could issue from us
with hope of being better than we were.

The Top Ten Reasons Why I Take Notes at Poetry

11. When I'm listening to 20 poets in a row,
it's hard to give them all the quality of attention
I'm going to want from them. Writing name and title
punctuates the flow, like locks on an English river.

10. To remind myself that the next three minutes
might be worth remembering for the rest of my life.
My note is a pin to fix that butterfly in my memory.

9. Ideas for new poems of my own. I don't have
to write the first poem on a given subject,
or the best, just one that's unmistakably mine.

8. A great line. I write it down to
consider it later, figure out why I liked it,
try for more of that in my own work.
Or maybe someday, when I'm a thousand
miles away, I'll just steal *that* line.

7. Sometimes I mishear a phrase
and think it would be fun to combine
what I thought I heard with what was
actually said. Or someone misreads their own
words in an interesting way—like the guy who
read "Miranda" before correcting it to
"meander" and I thought "Write that down,"
and someday in a poem of mine you'll see
the phrase "meandering Miranda warning."

6. If the cops ask where I was on March 22nd,
2004, I can say, "Bellingham, watching Karen
Finneyfrock; she was awesome, she did haiku,
she did Butterfly House, she got an encore.

The only thing she didn't do was the Orgasm poem—
I wonder why?" And the bad cop will tell me
not to leave town, but his heart won't be in it.

5. But suppose I'm doing three to five in
a place of standup guys while my public defender
is appealing that meandering Miranda warning
and I can't get to poetry readings any more;
I'll have my wife bake my note-cards into
a cake and I'll lick the chocolate lovingly,
reliving these evenings when I was as free
as my verse; and I'll put faces to the names
and almost hear the voices of people
who came out at night to gather in
odd-shaped rooms and share a little—
maybe of themselves, maybe of the persons
they'd have liked to be, and it will be just swell,
especially the double chocolate cake.

4. Or maybe the day will come
when the fabric of the state has been
by lies stretched so very thin that it
can't support the weight even of
one poet telling the truth in public,
and they outlaw poetry gatherings.

Or maybe not gatherings, maybe
they just outlaw *speaking* at gatherings,
and we come and sit in silence
to commemorate all that has been lost,
and I'll pass around my note-cards and you'll
all read them and here and there think
"I remember that," or "I wish I knew
what *that* was all about." I'm glad I'm
old; the future doesn't look too good.

3. And the day *will* come
when I can't get out to poetry any more.
Maybe we won't be able to afford a car,
or gas; maybe it'll be the nursing home
my daughter started threatening
when she was eight. I hope it's not
my eyes... but maybe I'd get someone

to read my cards to me, and they'd ask,
"What was Mike McGee like?"
and I'd try to describe Mike
how he looked like he should be carrying
a war-axe and bickering with Legolas
all the way to Lothlorien, how his poetry
was brilliant and hilarious, often
at the same time—and he liked pudding,
and running made him sad.

Someday someone will make a movie
about Mike McGee, and it will be one of
funniest films ever made, and one of
the saddest, and most inspiring
and life-affirming. And for a minute,
in my blindness and my vagueness it would
be as if Mike was in the room with us and I'd think,
"I wish just one more time before I die I could
hear Mike make the blue-whale noise."

2. You don't always get the chance that night
to tell someone how much you like their stuff;
then when you see them three weeks later,
you can't remember what it was you liked,
and it defeats the purpose to say, "You there!
I really admired that unmemorable poem you did
a few weeks ago, whatever your name is."

1. There's a poet named Marita O'Neill
from Portland, Maine who talks about when
a dog barks, sometimes all they're saying is,
"I'm a dog; I'm here." (I know I have that right;
it's on my card from 2/20/03, Beat Night,
The Press Room, Portsmouth, NH.)

My notecards are proof, my way of saying,
I'm Jack, I'm here, and I'm listening.
Woof! **Woof! WOOF**!

Fava Beans (& Sour Grapes)

There's a moment in "Silence of the Lambs"
when Hannibal Lecter is talking about
eating someone's liver sauteed with fava beans,
and washing it down with a nice chianti.
Everybody else in the theater was thinking,
"Eeeuw, gross," but me? all I registered was,
"Hmmm, a nice chianti, that sounds good."
But that's *my* obsession talking.

Hannibal and I share an acquired taste
most Americans can't understand.
We could have some great conversations
talking about our predilection
the direction that we turn for sustenance—
I refer, of course, to our subscriptions
to *Poetry* (the magazine).

Do you remember seeing it?
In "Silence of the Lambs"?
the sole indulgence permitted him,
displayed tactfully in a corner
of his pathologically sterile cell?
artifact so obviously harmless that
the authorities would permit it even
to a psycopath in a goalie mask.

But an object at the same time
so counter to American values
that the filmmaker could use it to say,
"See how unlike you is this man?
Do you understand now
how far above yours
is his mind?
Do you feel the *dread* yet?"
Poetry (the magazine) must have blown the whole
hoarded 20th century advertising budget
on that succulent product placement.

That was probably the only copy
most people have ever seen.
"Poet's Market" reported that *Poetry* had
a "press run of 10,000 for 7,000
subscribers, of which 53% are libraries."
That puts Hannibal and me in an elite group of
thirty-two hundred and ninety individual subscribers
worldwide—jeez, there's probably more people
than that who've tasted human flesh.

You have to suspect that a lot of the other
thirty-two hundred and eight-eight
have been published in *Poetry*—
which would suggest that the American Poetry
that the magazine has kept simmering
is a taste acquired only by a select few,
a closed shop of working poets
reading each other, writing for each other,
drawing their artistic sustenance
from their own kind.
Smelling Evian on each other.

But maybe, like the Donner Party,
Poetry should be applauded
just for surviving in a hostile environment,
purveying its unwanted wares
like a flea market on the outskirts
of the last stop on the gravy train.

The little menu items in "Poet's Market"
usually include a few hors d'oeuvres from past issues.
Poetry offers this, from a 1915 issue:

> *Let us go then, you and I,*
> *When the evening is spread out against the sky*
> *Like a patient etherized upon a table;*
> *Let us go, through certain half-deserted streets…*

Their stewardship of American Poetry
goes back a long way,
they bring a lot to the table;
but I've begun to wonder
exactly what procedure
that patient is on that table *for*.

If we're talking stewardship here,
Poetry is like the steward
who buried the talents in a safe place
by the dark of the moon—maybe
the same night Hannibal was out there
planting bones and skulls, grim, pathetic
remnants of an esoteric feeding.

Is it too late for a resurrection?
Maybe not; maybe *Poetry* could initiate
some kind of outlaw outreach program,
in between the poems and the criticism,
one poem a month—maybe even this
particular piece—perhaps with a disclaimer:
"We are unable to assent completely to this poem,
yet those that like this kind of thing
might find this the kind of thing they like."
Failing that, I'd suggest
offering gifts with each subscription.
Maybe T-shirts, with lines from favorite poets
(if you don't have a favorite poet,
one will be provided);
or food—food is always welcome;
maybe some really good fava beans,

a nice chianti.

24/7

In an interview back in his *Conan* days,
Schwarzenegger was asked what
made it all worthwhile, the hours
of pumping metal, the iron discipline
of the gym and the table.

Asked in a way that made it all
seem sad; freakish and distorted.
He said, "A lot of people have
achievements and accomplishments
dey can be proud of;

you go to deir office, dere's
a diploma on da vall. You go to deir home
dere's an Oscar on da mantelpiece,
or a bowling trophy—or both.
My achievement is my body,

and I get to carry it around vit me
tventy-four seven." Well, he probably
didn't actually say 24/7, I don't think
it was a word yet, but if it had been,
it's the word he would have used.

And he didn't say it braggadocio,
it came out almost wistful, apologetic,
as though he had asked himself the same
question many times, and even he
wasn't certain his answer was

good enough. I had read the interview
from an endomorph perspective,
expecting it to make him look
like the mental defective
I was certain that he was,

but I came away respecting him,
the way I might respect a roofer,
or a bricklayer or baseball player,
anyone who was serious about their work
and had some insights about it to share.

I thought about Arnold recently
while listening to yet another
can't-take-it-with-you riff, *you don't see
hearses pulling Uhaul trailers*. Yes,
the Governator does get to carry his body

around 24-7, to meetings of his cabinet,
lording it over all us desk-bound girly-men,
who can't see it, but we know it's there, and that
any time he wants to he can strip off his shirt
and expose his upper body, hard and proud,

ridged and veined like the fiercest erection
we ever had. But even ectomorphs
like Arnold don't get to take it
with them when they die;
nobody does. Well maybe

not quite nobody. Me, for example.
I have certain poems memorized. I was
the architect, I laid the bricks for the gym,
and I worked those poems as though they
were the quadriceps of my consciousness

and I was mainlining anabolic steroids,
and now they're part of me, 24-7.
And maybe someday, after we both
have died, I'll bump into Arnold on
the other side, and he'll ask me what

I did with my time on earth.
I won't even try to tell him, I'll do
what a writer is supposed to do,
I'll strip off my ectoplasmic shirt
and I'll show him this poem.

And I'll say,
"*Nngghh!*
Who da girly man
now,
bitch?"

Reflections on Retirement
OR
Ode to My Snooze Button

I indulged myself today:
I hit the snooze button.
Just a couple times, nothing
excessive, nothing decadent.
Just enough to remind myself that
I don't have to be anywhere
at any particular time.
Not today. Not most days.

The alarm goes off; I sigh,
like a long-haul trucker
at a rest area urinal.
My eyes closed, like his,
I grope for the snooze button.
In the poetry slam of pleasures,
this is nine-six, nine-seven.

My mother always had to call me
three-four times to get me up for school.
"I'm sick," I'd say, pull the pillow over my head,
roll over and go back to sleep. Eventually
she'd play on my sense of fairness.
"Get up and have some breakfast," she'd say.
If you still feel sick, you can stay home."
And every day, I'd fall for it.

When I went off to prep school at fourteen
it was touch-and-go until I learned
to place the clock across the room
so I'd have to get out of bed to turn it off.
And that the next, wrenching move had to be
in some direction other than back to bed.
Wrenching.

All my working years,
my first act of the day a violence upon myself,
that wrenching, like the seventy-ninth sit-up
of the fourth set. Getting up earlier and earlier

to beat the traffic, the sound of the alarm
the single most odious sound in the universe—

you want to torture me? Tie me to a chair
and set off an alarm across the room.
Three minutes max, I'll give up everything I know,
where the gold is buried, where my wife is hiding,
my kids, the address of the lawyer holding the letter
to be opened in the event of my death—
I'll *volunteer* that one.

My first sponsor once said to me,
"To cultivate humility, Jackie, every day
do two things you don't want to do."
I said, "Tim, I got it covered:
I get up and go to work."

All those years,
all those wrenching mornings,
all those dead-end jobs.
The best you could say for them was
marginally more interesting than daytime TV.
What keeps you going? What keeps you
from blowing your brains out?
Only the hope that maybe someday,
things will get better.

Well this bulletin just in:
Someday is here.
I still set the alarm for five o'clock.
But I don't get up at five o'clock.
I just gently stroke the snooze button, thinking,
"I hope this is as good for you as it is for me,"
and I burrow back into the warm womb
of the blankets thinking, *"This is
the payoff, this the magnificent reality,
this is what I worked for all those years."*

And I go back to sleep. For nine minutes,
until the alarm goes off again,
and the whole process starts over.
How many times do I do this?
I do it till I'm good and ready.

The snooze button:
it's the clitoris of life.

After Interviewing Hundreds of Men, Miss Manners Answers All Your Questions About Men's Room Etiquette

The First Great Commandment is
Thou shalt not make the slightest move,
however innocent, they could interpret
as expressing interest in another man's...
how shall I say this?.......*member*.

Choosing your urinal is half the game. If there's
only one urinal, there's no choice, and therefore no
exposure—except be quick if they're lined up behind.

If there are two urinals
then each is as good as the other;
but you must turn your shoulder very slightly
from the fixture not taken. The slightness
of the gesture is important: this is
not fear, but nuance, delicacy.
Even if no one's there when you arrive,
calibrate the attitude of shoulder
so you don't have to move a millimeter
should someone come to take the other one.

If there are three urinals,
then things get more complex.
A good rule is you never stand
beside another man if there's a choice.
Rule two, never make the next man in
stand next to you. With three therefore,
the only time you go the middle's
when the other two are taken.

And if you've no choice
but a position between two other men,
hunch your shoulders up and go in deep,
hold your breath, gaze straight ahead,
and think of... waterfalls.

If there are four or five, and fairly busy—
an Eastwood movie, say, or Bruins game—
go for the end position if it's there.
Beside is always better than between.

But, if there are more than five or six,
and mostly empty, don't go to the end,
it makes you look like a wimp;
and although this is always an ordeal,
you must not let it show. One position
left or right of middle is ideal.

Idiosyncrasies in general are to be avoided.
Like this new phenomenon
of men for whom the fly is not enough,
but they must undo their pants entirely
to get their business done;
the men Miss Manners talked with asked,
"Are they trying to tell us something?
Like, *'They just don't make these flies*
big enough any more, do they buddy?
Oh, I guess you don't have my problem.'
Or are they wearing women's underpants?"

What about that little sag men do
with their knees, as they unzip the fly,
as though preparing to lift something
really heavy? My men consider this
within the bounds of etiquette,
unconscious hyperbole
that injures no one.

And if there's a soggy
cigarette butt in your line of fire,
targeting it does not count as
an idiosyncrasy to be avoided;
Indeed, some men describe it
as a gender imperative:

women get to make babies;
men play Battleship with Marlboros.
It's okay—praise the Lord
and pass the ammunition.

The last thing always is
to wash your hands. Hmph.
If men had any sense of reverence,
they'd also wash their hands
before they touched themselves.

THE DERVISH & THE ELEPHANT

On the Indian subcontinent
sometimes an elephant
goes rogue. Always a male,
but that's not the point.
(At least it's not my point, here.)

One day the elephant awakes
with maybe excess of testosterone,
and asks the existential question:
"*Why? Why* am I doing this?
Why don't I do what *I* want to do?"

As if in a power plant
serving some great city
the nuclear reactor
suddenly developed a mind of its own
and water couldn't cool it any more

or as if a convict, muscles
hard from years of breaking up
big rocks on the chain gang, were
unexpectedly pardoned, or even
better, ordered to be on a plane

leaving for Vegas at half past two,
what are the odds that he'd say,
"I was kinda lookin' forward
to bustin' up some more
big rocks today?"

Or a systems analyst
suddenly perceived that he stood astride
the corporate revenue stream, thought, "Geez,
what if I tried to hold this update hostage,
bargain for some job security…?"

An elephant off the reservation
like that's supremely dangerous
because entirely unpredictable
without even the common
horse-sense of self-preservation.

The dilemma is that he's extremely
valuable as well, someone's property,
so killing him would make people nervous.
Instead they say, "This is a case for a dervish;"
and they find one to bring to the elephant.

(That makes it sound easy; fact is,
persuading dervishes to travel any distance,
do anything but follow the bizarre insistence
of their inner voices requires extraordinary
tact, is only marginally less difficult

than negotiating with elephants direct.
It must be that centuries of coexistence
with elephant and dervish—
and, dare I say it, British—
have taught Indian villagers a trick or two.)

The dervish stands before the elephant.
Elephant thinks, "What's this here? Why
doesn't he fear me, like everyone else?"
Dervish and elephant stare deep
into one another's eyes, until elephant

goes to sleep, forgets to be mad,
returns to a state of sublimation,
is led back peacefully to his vocation,
dragging huge logs through jungles,
or whatever it is that elephants do.

Why do dervishes have this effect?
Nobody knows, except maybe the dervish
and perhaps the elephant, and neither
of them is talking, though we suspect
that the elephant remembers.

There are, however, theories.
My favorite is that when the elephant's
gaze is held by those dervish eyes,
it's like a Vulcan mind-meld, in which
the elephant learns he's up against a craziness

greater far than his own, and wakes up
to the fact that on the Richter scale
of madness, Man is Krakatoa,
and Elephant can't even crack a teacup.
Everything settles in place once more,

and in that instant, elephant feels
naked without that hook in his ear—
which he now perceives as a rather dear
ornament, a sort of dangling earring
with a little man on the end of it,

and quite a sane and pleasant man at that,
compared to the entity in front of him now.
He thinks, 'Actually, I sort of miss dragging
humungous logs through my muddy jungle.
I want to go home.'

And as mysteriously as the world hiccuped
in the first place, the nuclear reactor responds
to control. There'll be no China Syndrome
today, no Three Mile Island; just technicians
mistrusting their gauges and clocks.

The con gets to beat up on his rocks;
the analyst tugs at the lobe of his ear,
shakes his head as if to help it clear,
goes back to work; is not in charge;
the dervish goes back to just being at large.

Lucretius on 128

Tire rolls forward; hubcap spins.
At any instant the whole top
half is moving forward,
bottom back.
What of the single point
at dead center?

If points above are moving one way
points below the other
logic demands one single point
that doesn't rotate at all.
This is what I aspire to:
the still point at the center.

While everybody spins their wheels
they know where to find me.
I stand out like the face
in the crowd at the tennis match
in the Hitchcock Movie
staring at his prey

while every other face
follows the ball
back and forth, back and forth,
till your eye is irresistibly drawn
to the one still point,
the murderer's face....

But how can there be
a still point at the center?
Attached to a point above that's moving
forward and one below moving back,
how can a point not choose between,
not go with one, yet not be torn?

Only one answer possible:
nothing really is attached. It is as
physicists and Buddhists and Lucretius
assert: every object atoms and void,
night sky, ocean of darkness,
here and there a point of light.

It is we impose upon this ocean
names to satisfy our need
for the illusion of understanding:
call this frequency "black;"
call this black surface "road;"
call this road "128;"

call this town "Burlington;"
call this direction "forward;"
call this collection of atoms "me."
And it all works until two turns later
you realize that although
you know where *you* are—

here—
you don't know where *here* is,
or what this new black surface is called.
In the glove compartment a map
and on that map a point
that represents where you are now.

But your point has no name,
white area among meandering lines.
Oh, the people in the houses
know where *here* is
but they don't know who *you* are
so you have no expectation

they might help you.
It's very dark, you're low on gas.
It's some consolation that
the roadmap in the glove compartment
is folded perfectly;
but not much.

My friend Jack the Marine once said
that he had wanted so badly to be
one of those people who knew,
while everybody else was running around
in circles, exactly what to do,
that he became one of them.

And now he knows those people
only feel alive when there's
a crisis running, pay terrible prices
when it's over. Whirlpool isn't
whirlpool unless it has a hole
at center; but a hole isn't

anything at all without a whirlpool.
Lucretius was right:
all there is is atoms and void.
The still point at the center that
refuses and refutes connection
is void.

They're Dragging the Lake for Dennis

Perhaps he will come laughing from the woods,
breathing, and wreaking some barbaric pun.
But no—Dennis is dead.

He drowned in the dark, in cold
October water in New Hampshire.
There was no moon, but there were stars,
above a heavy ground-mist.

He went out, for a lark, upon the lake,
in a rowboat that was there.
The boat looked worthy, but it leaked.
Such are the gaps in our assumptions;
so often do we live, or die, by fluke.

He called for help and was heard,
heard and ignored by the people
in the cabins on the shore,
warm and dry, in the light,
breathing and saying, "While you're up..."
"Just kids," they thought,
"screwing around. (And if they're not,
then may they pay the price for all the kids
who ever screwed around, disturbed the peace,
and broke our cottage windows in off-season.)"

He swam off, probably, with full intent to live,
intention reconsidered very soon
as cold exhaustion siphoned his resolve.
And then the question,
suddenly and finally demanding,
"Is it worth it? Yes or no, and now."
Is it worth one more stroke?

> And for each stroke the question is the same,
> the price keeps escalating.
> An auction, piece by piece, of a matching set,
> worthless to him if broken up, of strokes.
> And death is bidding from capital unlimited,
> and to unending time,
> and taunting, "Now, or later?"

Twice he helped us move, doing a man's work;
we still owe him for the second time.
His favorite joke was mispronouncing.
His delight was so infectious that you had to laugh
when he'd say "doag-nuts," or "afleection."
Always he referred to the pastor as "Monster" Norton.
He did a creditable Boris Karloff,
and for Halloween he had a Groucho Marx mask.
He received Communion yesterday.
He was a generous and gentle boy, not very tall,
and they will find his slender body soon,
because the lake is small.

We shall be expected at the house.
Library books to be returned, and such.
The grandmother, without her "Dinnis,"
will need someone to watch with her,
shouting consolation at her discount hearing-aid.
A roomful of teenage squalor to be cleaned;
debts and respects to be paid.

And tonight, while his lovely sisters weep,
the monsignor lights a candle,
and cottagers rest in easy sleep,
knowing there's one less vandal.

A Prayer for John Fernandez

In the late 70s, radical Catholics were actually
studying the Bible—a truly radical idea.
The Church had never trusted us around the Bible,
like those warnings on the back of a TV set:
"We strongly suggest that you not open this up
if you don't know fuck-all about it..."
I was part of a Bible discussion group led by
a young, tall, thin-as-a-rail curate with the brooding
good looks of the young Montgomery Clift.
The women of the parish had dubbed him
"Father What-a-Waste."

We had people in that group were
always trying to trap Father into heresy.
He was a Vatican 2 person,
all about forgiveness, reconciliation,
disciple of John XXIII's aborted attempt
to open the windows of the Church.
He had an air of sad sanctity, as though
wearing a hair-shirt under cassock and collar.
I remember somebody once saying of him,
"For one who has no darkness in himself, he has
the best understanding of other people's darkness
that I've ever come across."

One time Father was visibly upset
when he arrived at our Bible group.
One of the women prodded him gently,
and at length he admitted that he'd just caught
a boy to whom he had entrusted his keys
borrowing quarters from the Coke machine.
He felt deeply betrayed. Someone asked—
with only the slightest hint of taunting—
if Father had forgiven the boy.
After a long pause he said,
"Give me three days."

In another of these Bible sessions
we talked about the forgiveness of sin;
how could murderers be forgiven, rapists?

Father saw their crimes as products
of a long string of decisions of which
maybe the only decision that involved
free will was the first one, and maybe
in God's eyes that first decision
had no moral content, yet once made,
determined everything that followed.

Somebody demanded to know what
Father's definition of sin was,
and I wrote down his exact words,
because I had a vague but urgent sense
that something important had been left out.

I went home and studied it and came back
the next week primed to nail Father.
I read him back his definition and he nodded;
I asked, "Then what's the difference between a sin
and a life-mistake, like taking the wrong job,
or marrying the wrong person?" (As I look back
it's apparent that both of these examples were issues
I was just beginning to deal with in my own life.)

Father What-a-Waste answered, "There is no difference."
That shut me up real quick, plus gave me something
to ponder down all the years since.

I also knew Father from CCD, Catholic
Sunday School, but held on Monday nights,
the longest hour of my week,
trying to pass on what few nuggets
of truth I had picked up along the way
to a handful of hormonal public school boys
who saw my classroom as a holding cell.
The only way I could maintain the illusion
that any learning whatever was taking place
was by sending my discipline problems
to Father What-a-Waste.

One night when they were giving me
a really bad time, I gave them an ultimatum,
the next kid who opened his mouth
would be sent to Father's office.
And of course the next kid that did was
the best kid in the class, John Fernandez;
all the hard kids had the street smarts
to know I wasn't kidding.

John didn't want to leave my room,
I had to haul him out physically.
Father happened to be patrolling the hall
at that moment, took possession of John from me
seconds before I might actually have struck him.

Father What-a-Waste got his handsome picture
in the paper recently over a report that the institute
that deals with pedophile priests had discharged him
as an untreatable sociopath, and that has set me
thinking again about him, and about the difference
between a sin and a bad life-decision.

I know he must have done the kind of things
he was accused of; there's no room for any
mistaken identity, no legal technicalities
to compromise my judgment.

I know my church was guilty
of a hideous and hypocritical mistake
in handling this and other cases like it,
a mistake and an institutional sin
and a crime against nature.
I'm thinking it'll take about a hundred years
of penance and mortification and amending its ways,
confessing that it doesn't know
fuck-all about human sexuality
before this church can presume to
any moral authority whatever.

And I still believe that Father What-a-Waste
was a good and maybe even holy person

when I knew him—though the reason he was so
understanding of the darkness in others was
he did indeed have a darkness of his own,
growing very slowly, like a prostate
cancer he'd been told that he could heal
with magical thinking and organic foods,
a cancer that eventually consumed
his entire beautiful spiritual being.

And I wonder what that first
and almost innocent decision was
that sent him down his terrible road
to untreatability.

I pray for him every day. I pray
for all the priests, especially the many
who never laid a hand on anyone;
so humiliated, so unjustly.
The worst kind of guilt-by-association,
yet the most natural.

I pray for the victims;
it must have been as if
God Himself was abusing you.
I hope you get enough out of the Church
that you never have to worry about money again.
I hope you may finally be able to forgive—
maybe not the Institution that enabled him,
but at least the poor sick bastard who violated you—
because only then will you know you're healing.

And I say a special prayer for John Fernandez,
whom I had to drag out of his seat, and for all
the discipline problems from my CCD class
that I handed over to Father What-a-Waste.

Most prayers are aimed at things
we cannot know about the future;
This one is for things that
I don't want to know
about the past.

British Addresses: an Introduction

My last job was for a company whose main business was creating data bases for direct marketers. So when you got that annoying phone call right at suppertime, I was, if not responsible, at least complicit.

Our clients were some of the biggest banks in the country, and insurance companies here and abroad. For a couple of years, I was the guy on the UK desk. British addresses were different enough from ours to demand some degree of specialization.

My job required a great deal of quality control, which meant detailed visual inspection of random hundreds of individual addresses before shipping a data base. In the course of those inspections, I learned that British addresses are not always as prosaic as ours. Sometimes the British name their houses: "Squirrel's Leap," "Retina Cottage," "Podnods." Sometimes the address can sound like directions: "The New House by the Green Near Knutsford." I started writing down addresses that I considered especially colorful, and posting them on the wall of my cubicle.

Eventually my addresses started calling out to me, begging to have their stories told. They promised that if I would simply riff on their elements, poems would present themselves. So I tried it.

In those days, I was reading in the open mike at the Cantab (Central Square, Cambridge, Massachusetts) every week. My British Address poems were pretty popular, went a long way toward making what reputation I have today. It was often suggested that I bring out a chapbook of them, but that would have put my job in jeopardy—perhaps the company I worked for as well. The Statute of Limitations has now expired on that.

Lest you get any bright ideas, understand that once I had gotten what I wanted from a given address, I was scrupulous about changing enough of the rest of it to render it undeliverable. Other than that precaution, the addresses in the poems are real; of the elements in play, not one was invented by me.

Following are some of the British Addresses that, in my opinion, came closest to making good on their promise.

Mr. Dick

Mr. Alan Dick / 21 Rederech Crescent / Musselburgh / Lanarkshire

Dear Mr. Dick,

If I remember my David Copperfield,
there was a character named Mr. Dick.
Are you at all like him?
Maybe you have larks in Lanarkshire,
fly kites above Rederech Crescent,
give sage advice to the strapping,
stolid inhabitants of Musselburgh.

There used to be, here in the States,
on the telly, a character called Mr. Bill.
He would cry Ooooh Noooooo and we would
howl with laughter—curiously difficult now
to explain precisely why. Perhaps,
Mr. Dick, you're more like Mr. Bill.

Mr. Bill had a friend named Mr. Fingers.
In a way, you might be more like Mr. Fingers.
Have you heard of Mr. Bill and Mr. Fingers?
Perhaps you've met Mr. Fingers?
Were you introduced? Did they say,
Mr. Dick, I'd like you to meet Mr. Fingers?
And did you hit it off right away?

St. Agnes

Frances Mary Parker/ The Turks Head / St. Agnes / Isle of Scilly

Dear Fanny,

Once, with Christmas coming, my wife asked me
to look around downtown and see if I could find
a Turk's head. I said, "Ten, twenty years ago,
along the waterfront, maybe. But these days
you can't even tell an ethnic joke."

Bada-bim, bada-boom. But seriously,
Frances, tomorrow, January twentieth,
is the Eve of Saint Agnes. Legend says
that if a virgin performs certain ceremonies
on that night she'll be granted a vision
of her future husband.

Today it's so cold here he'd probably appear
in a ski mask. There's a catch to everything.
Maybe if my first wife had done the mumbo-jumbo,
she'd have seen me. A catch to everything.
And what about the Virgin Mary? What virtual
reality might have visitated her?

Ah, Frances, get out your candles
and your incense, do tomorrow night
whatever it is that virgins do, and if
all that shows up is a Turk's head in
a ski mask, don't write it off as Scilly;
the point is not that someone else
love you. Thank the saint, instead,
that you live in a place whose name
sounds like "I love."

Miss L. Wild & Saint Anthony

Miss L. Wild / St. Anthony's Lodge / Horsley Lane / Coxbench / Derbyshire

Dear Miss Wild,

Over here, if you saw "L. Wild"
in a phone book, you'd know it was
a single woman trying to disguise
the fact she lives alone;
but you choose to be addressed

as Miss, you give the game away.
This suggests conflict. And what
does "L" stand for? what is it about
your Christian name that renders you
reluctant to reveal it?

You titillate; a little mystery
where none should be.
I'll call you Lorelei;
Lorelei Wild of Derbyshire.
Do people wear derbies in Derbyshire?

When you're making love with the man who doesn't
live with you, won't let you take his name,
do you wear a derby then? like the woman
in Unbearable Lightness of Being?
Maybe L stands for Love, or Lightness...

What woman, if she could
design her own address, would opt
for Horsley Lane in Coxbench?
Maybe you never had a choice,
you're trapped, like a lone hiker

in the Wilderness, whose foot
has gotten lodged in a cleft
of unforgiving granite...
But one might just as well ask what
Saint Anthony is doing there.

Or do you Brits pronounce it,
like "Sinjin," "Sin Inthiny?"
And what dichotomies of spirit,

if you do, does that betray?
If I were a saint I'd like to be

the missionary to the Whores;
to pray with all my soul and half
my heart, "Protect me from temptation,"
when maybe what I should be praying is,
"Protect temptation from me."

Oh, to hear just one of their
confessions! to forgive one juicy
misstep after another; to have them say
when I am dead, "He gave great ear"
to those who give great head…

We learned a rhyme as children:
"Blessed Saint Anthony, look around;
something's lost and can't be found."
Which said, miraculously things turned up
sometimes. Maybe L is for lost—

you advertise your wild side
but conceal how lost you feel.
Ah, Lorelei, don
your derby and sit tight.
The whores and cocks will go

their merry way without you;
they always have, they always will.
Nothing is unbearable, really;
we're all whores, one way or another.
And sometimes whoring gets

a little boring, that's all. But
somewhere out there is a real saint,
summoning anyone who knows she's lost.
Until you hear that gentle call,
stay put; you are securely lodged.

When Great Detectives Get Together

N. P. Sherlock / Thames Valley Police / Cowley Police Station / Oxford Road / Oxford

My dear Sherlock,

One cannot help but wonder
how you get along with
the irascible Inspector Morse,
also of the Thames Valley Police.

If a layman might presume
to warn a peace officer,
I caution you never to say,
"Elementary, my dear Morse."

Morse would never indulge
in direct vulgarity, but he might find
a way to say, in quotation marks
audible even without the hand signals,
"The Americans have a curious expression
for such revelations. They say,
'No shit, Sherlock.'"

And leave your pipe at home.
One whiff and Morse will curl his lip
and sniff, "Must you?"

And if you play the violin, but badly,
don't bring it to the office to help you think;
Morse will descend on you like Belushi
and smash the instrument over your desk.
And not even say, "I'm sorry. I had to do that."

As to your rumored drug habit, I suggest
thou get thee to a program, fast.
Morse is not entirely without compassion,
but has little tolerance for good coppers
gone bad—or much of anything else.

No, I think you're well out of
your red-headed league here, Sherlock.
Go back to Baker Street, back to chasing
Moriarty, who—here's a tip—
has taken up residence
on the holodeck
of the Starship Enterprise.

If you insist on
hanging around Thames Valley
you'll come away with nothing
but re-Morse.

British Address #31 — Goodfellow

George Goodfellow / 74 Broomfield Avenue / Redditch / Aberdeenshire

Dear George,

When I started writing these little riffs,
I made an ironclad rule for myself
not to make fun of people's names.
If you don't like what your address
says about you, you can always
move house; but changing your name—
that's a very California thing to do.
We wouldn't do it in Boston,
and I bet that it's considered
aberrational in Aberdeenshire.

But sometimes a name comes along
and I say to myself
like Bill Murray in Ghostbusters,
"That wasn't actually a rule,
it was more like a guideline;"
or Christopher Lloyd in Back to the Future:
"Then I figured, 'What the hell…'"

George, yours is one of those names.

Not that I'm going to make fun,
and not that it's actually even *your* name—
see, I used to have a friend named George Goodfellow.
He was from Dorchester, not Aberdeenshire.
I introduced him to my wife once,
and as we chatted he told us
about the living room set
he had just bought for his wife.

He bought it on credit,
he didn't know how he'd pay for it, but,
"What the hell? Life's too short, Jackie."
He said that a couple of times.

All the way home, Joan kept chuckling.
"He's like a character in Bunyan:
George Goodfellow: 'Life's too short, Jackie.'"
The only Bunyan character I could think of was
his blue ox Babe, but I kept my mouth shut.

Years later now,
George Goodfellow of Aberdeenshire,
I'm writing to ask you a favor.
They say you Scots are pretty
circumspect with a shilling;
but I want you to say a Presbyterian prayer
for my friend and your profligate
namesake black-sheep cousin,
the late George Goodfellow
of the Fields Corner Group.

Then go into your front parlor
and look at the furniture.
Would it make your wife happy
to see a new sofa in there?

Probably you've got a rule
against buying things on credit.
But ask yourself, is it really a rule?
Or is it more of a guideline?

Then say these words:
"What the hell."
Because you know what, Georgie?
Life's too short.
It's just too fucking short.

"I came humbly, hat in hand, to literary America. I didn't ask for much; I had a book or two to publish. I didn't expect to make money at it. I saw myself at the tail end of a great glory. I was very moved by the books I had read in school, and I brought an offering to the altar."

—Saul Bellow

"Certain death; small chance of success; what are we waiting for?"

—Gimli

Cartalk III—the Karma Doors

First, the key wouldn't work in the driver-side.
Next, the door-handle came off
on the passenger side.
Then the driver's door denied me
when I tried opening it from *in*side.

Made me wonder what sin I'd committed
in what prior incarnation
to have so much karma.

As long someone's with me, I'm okay.
I get in, reach across
and let them in. Once we arrive
where we're going, they get out
and walk around and let me out.
Somebody's roundabout way of showing
no man is an island, maybe.
Not exactly limo,
but no problemo, baby.

Problemo comes when I'm someplace alone
and have to wriggle across to the passenger door,
shoving my detritus from seat to floor,
like some clumsy Michigan militiaman,
bones riddled with arthritis, playing at war.
They don't make cars like this any more.

Oh, I know we need to replace
this caricature of car,
but the time's not right just yet—
promises to keep, and all—
unless we could get
someone to buy this one
for more than just its parts.
And it does run,
bless its battered heart,
it's got miles to go, it would
be good for someone who could just
get in and out of it—
Houdini, maybe.

Picture me saying to some wary prospect,
"Sure we can take it for a spin,
Harry. And to sweeten the deal,
I'm going to bring you in through
the hatchback, so you get a feel
for all the cargo space."
Say that with a straight face.

And to be perfectly honest,
the car is cosmetically daunted.
One time Peter fixed...
something under the hood that wanted
lubricating, or perhaps was haunted,
and we were test-driving,
and he pulled over and called out,
"Hey, Louie, I've got a car for you,"
and Lou looked dubious and said,
"It's not *that* one, is it?" and Peter laughed
and said, "No, no, no." And true,
the car was idling a little rough,
but I don't think Peter had to laugh,
and one No would have been enough:
Louie knows problemo when he sees one.

The doors work well when it's warm and dry.
They must be riddled with rust.
But on some days that are bitter cold
they amaze by opening first try—
but then they won't stay closed
because the spring on the latch is frozen.
All you do on those
occasions is turn the heat up high
and hold the door with one hand,
steer with the other
until the spring thaws;
don't break any traffic laws,
but no cause for concern, my brother.

But did I mention that the heater's gone?
This is starting to sound like
an automotive Twilight Zone,
or a Zen koan illuminating
the connectedness of all things.
No wonder the Japanese
are good at automaking:
all those years of contemplating
the sound of one windshield wiper scraping.
I need a shogun riding shotgun.

The day is going to come
when I can't get out of the car at all:
a new spin on the word in-*car*-cerated.
They say that if you're ever knocked
off a bridge into deep water you should
roll your windows down and let the river in.
That equalizes pressure
and the door will open easily.
That's Plan B.

I think what we need to equalize
is time, so the car and I crap out
at exactly the same moment,
and all you'll have to do
is dig a hole in front of us
give us a shove
say a prayer or two
read that poem about love
cover us up and walk away
and pay a Dixieland band to play
Didn't He Ramble,
and at the first payphone call Triple-A
and tell them they
can take me off speed-dial

and keep the change.

The Death I Was Never Afraid of

My son-in-law Mark works for
an elder who says there are three
major lessons he's learned getting old:
1) never pass up a bathroom; 2) never let
an erection go to waste; and 3) never trust
a fart. Yeah, I thought it was funny too—
till it starts happening to you.

Real life, these days, is rife
with mournful realizations. When they
ask how I am, my stock answer is,
"The body is breaking down slowly—
but the important word is 'slowly.'"

But I don't like this breakdown,
however slow. I'm a guy who didn't think
I'd live to see twenty-five. I'd go out heroic
trying to rescue some little girl from some
hypothetical raging river; or ignominious,
drunk and asleep at the wheel. They'd all
say, "It was the way Jack'd've wanted to
go: doing the three things he loved best:
drinking, driving, and sleeping. (Pity
they're not a better combination.)"

What I was really shopping for was
a Thane of Cawdor death, one of which
they'd say, "Nothing in his life became him
like the leaving it." I was a martyr whose
only cause was, if you've got a blacklist
I wanna be on it. It wasn't enough to *burn*
my draft card, no, I had to mail it to the
White House. I was James Cagney
yelling, "Come and get me, coppers!"
and adding, "Please!"

Failing a worthy cause, I was prepared
to bypass revolution and go straight to
execution, my last words already written,
quote: I only regret that I have but one life
to give for… whatever. Unquote.

My lack of fear of death was based on
an implicit assumption that the manner
of one's death should be in some way
elective, to be chosen from a menu
of death options, none of which
could be called suicide.

And on that menu any death I wasn't
afraid of would be quick, like the one
Satchel Paige had in mind when asked
how he felt about flying; he said, "Airplanes
may kill you, but they ain't likely to *hurt* you."

Maybe it's an ethnic thing: Irish
fishermen, traditionally, never learned
to swim. It was a conscious choice:
a relatively quick death by drowning
preferable to the long, cold, and
probably hopeless swim for survival.
And those wonderful, thick wool
Clancy Brothers sweaters—guaranteed
to drag you to the bottom fast.

When Gabrielle's body broke down
under chemo and she shuffled off to
hospice, it wasn't what I'd been praying for
for her, but neither was it what I prayed
against.

Death doesn't scare me, but chemo
does, the more if it be doomed to fail.
And this breakdown of my own body,
however slow; cascading systems failure;
this is the death of a thousand cuts, death by
entropy. Death of a thousand goodbyes:
goodbye to alcohol, to cigarettes,
to jogging; to grilled cheese and bacon
sandwiches, peanut butter and bacon
sandwiches; to bacon, cheese, peanut butter;
potato chips, bananafana sundaes with
coffee ice cream; to ice cream; to coffee;

and to french fries, to baked potatoes
dripping with butter and sour cream
and chives—oh, wait: chives are OK.

I've said so many goodbyes already.

This is death by doctor's appointments
that get closer and closer together
until they simply squeeze out all living.
By the most important sign on the road
being the miles to the next rest area.
This is the death of dignity. Death
by stool sample, by prostate exam.

This death is a long, slow process,
not the death I signed up for. This is
not the death I was never afraid of.

When the Cholesterol Catches Up With Me

Lord, if there really is reincarnation, please,
I'd rather not come back if I don't have to.
Nothing else you might have planned
for me can be as good as this one was.
I feel like an old soul who got my dues
paid up the first half of this lifetime. Since
then it's been, as Raymond Carver put it,
"all gravy."

1.

This be the verse you grave for me:
Here he lies where he longed to be;
Home is the sailor, home from sea,
and the hunter, home from the hill.
—Robert Louis Stevenson

Those were the first lines of poetry that
memorized themselves within me after
childhood, as though I always knew that after
all the alarums and excursions would come
this peace.

2.

I don't much care what happens in the immediate
aftermath of my death; just please don't do anything
sad. Let there be parties—but not those parties
where guys like me stand around silent
because we can never figure out when it's
our turn to talk; throw a party like an open mike,
where people sign up and wait for their name to be called,
and everybody sits and listens, sipping coffee and tea.

Let there be jokes and stories—and music.
And let there be poetry. But most of all, let there be
listening—let this be an interlude of respect, with one
person at a time speaking, and everyone else
listening.

3. When my daughters were little we used to take them hiking
in the Blue Hills. They'd say "Where we going today?"
and we'd answer, "The Blue Hills," and they'd piss and moan,
"Not the Blue Hills *again*?" and we'd say, "Oh be quiet.
You know you love the Blue Hills," and they'd say,
"We *hate* the Blue Hills," and that would be that—

until we got to the Blue Hills,
and Megan Kathleen and Annie
would be out of the car and into the woods,
checking out frog ponds or lady slippers,
garter snakes, pine cones, toadstools or horse manure—
which they would pronounce *gross*!
in voices that sang with wonder—
and for the next two hours keeping the them
out of the poison ivy and within hailing distance
would be like squadron-commanding butterflies.

Once, on a wet day in early spring
when Annie was still in the back-pack,
the footing failed me going down a hill:
my muscles still remember the terrible
torque of their improvised response
to the unprecedented instruction from
my brain to twist in the instant of falling,
twist so as to land on my stomach
and hands, and not on my back and on
Annie, and Joan said that twist was
the greatest athletic achievement
of my life and I believe she was right—
so what if it's not a very high bar?

Several Septembers and a world of changes
and one personal ad later I met Carol
and on one of our early dates I took her hiking
up that same Hawk Hill, and at every point of
prospect we would pause to kiss and enjoy the view—
all haze and treetops to the cars on 128; maybe a hawk.
I suggested we move in together and she said no,
bad example for my girls. I digested that a few seconds,

wondering if I wouldn't be wise to hold out for a woman
with—ooooh, money? But Good Angel warned that I'd
end up kicking myself if I let this one get away,
so I said, "OK, then, let's get married."
And that was the wisest life-decision I ever made—
(though that bar's even lower than the first one).

4. I don't want to be buried: Burn my body.
Dump my ashes in a shoebox.
Take them to the Blue Hills. Wear boots.
Follow the Skyline Trail to Hawk Hill.
(If it's spring, watch out for rattlesnakes.)
Pass the box from hand to hand
and scatter me along the path.
No big ceremony. Chat among yourselves.

Why this? Because Fenway Park
probably wouldn't be available, and because
I think Walt Whitman got it right:

> *I bequeath myself to the dirt to grow from the grass I love,*
> *If you want me again look for me under your bootsoles.*
> *You will hardly know who I am or what I mean,*
> *But I shall be good health to you nevertheless...*

Do the scattering on your way up the hill,
so that on your way back down, you may truly
look for me under your bootsoles.

About the Author

Pictured above with his wife Carol (and an unidentified third party), Jack McCarthy is the author of *Say Goodnight, Grace Notes, New and Corrected Poems* (EM Press, 2003) and the poetry CD *By Gift Unearned* (EM Press, 2007), as well as five other volumes of poetry.

A retired working guy from Boston, McCarthy is a graduate of Phillips Exeter Academy and Dartmouth College, where he majored in Latin. He got serious about poetry late in life. He calls himself "a standup poetry guy;" others have called him "legend." He has been featured at venues all over the US, as well as in Canada and Europe. The Boston Globe has written, "In the poetry world, he's a rock star." Poet Stephen Dobyns has called him, "one of the wonders of contemporary poetry."

His poetry has been heard on NPR and has appeared, along with his essays, in numerous publications, including The Boston Globe, The Worcester Review, Rattle, and World Literature Today, and such anthologies as "The Spoken Word Revolution," "The Spoken Word Revolution Redux," and the very prestigious "Complete Idiot's Guide to Slam Poetry."

He has made it to the finals stage of the National Poetry Slam, won the haiku championship at the Individual World Poetry Slam, and represented Seattle at the Individual World Poetry Slam in 2011. He's an engaging minor character in the film "Slamnation."

He and the fabulous Carol have been living in the state of Washington since 2003. His website is www.standupoet.net.